# until i know.

Tabitha Musa

BookLeaf Publishing

India | USA | UK

Presentation by *BookLeaf Publishing*

Web: www.bookleafpub.com

E-mail: info@bookleafpub.com

ISBN: 9789360940485

First edition 2024

# Why do you write?

I could write endless verses,
Emotions pour out of my pores,
But I absorb as much as I release so sometimes
it feels like there is no release at all
But,
even still
I write to articulate that which I feel I cannot say
with my mouth.
I let it out through the medium of my five digits.
Letters on a page protect and save and do not
fade like the remnants of my thinkings

I'm always thinking...

# on the living room floor

I lie on the floor a lot.
There's something about the ground which
grounds me

Sometimes I look to the side,
Turning left or right,
But the natural inclination of one lying down
Is to look up

The ceiling becomes a canvas upon which I
paint a myriad imaginations,
My contemplations covering even the corners of
this skyward plain.

The line soon blurs between imagination and
inspiration,
Inspiration to aspiration
Until,
I'm filled with the prospect of potential to fulfil

I smile to myself, and slowly rise.
For I cannot lie on the floor any more

# The richest place on Earth

In the distance
Not too far off
I see a cemetery
And in the sunset of spring
The rows of stones and crosses
Look strangely serene
May they rest in peace

They say the richest place on Earth is graveyard
The soil made lush by the wealth of ideas taken
into the deep

As I squint at the stones
I can't help but hope
That their dreams didn't die with them

# At the end of time

People say that history repeats itself
And it's true
There is indeed nothing new
Under the sun that seems to shine
For an endless amount of time
Cycles cycle
And patterns pervade our day to day.
Like the ebb and flow of the sea,
We advance and we retreat
Change is continuity
So it would seem

But maybe there is something,
That's always present but sometimes presents
itself
That breaks the cycles of normality
Defies the definition of how things are "meant to
be"
What if the sea didn't retreat
And history didn't repeat
And the conflicts that consistently arise were to
subside
Truly. Once and for all.

At some point the sun will cease to shine

And at that time no thing will remain except one

Love.

# "Just friends"

We were never "together" but never apart
And slowly
Our minds became entwined
Under the guise of just friends
And I didn't realise in time to hit the brakes

Was it a mistake to get so close to the flames?
I don't know
But I would say
That I learnt so much about my life and about
life itself
Amid the journey of attachment and the pain of
separating.

Would I do it again?

Perhaps it's already too late.

# Letters to my ex

I still write letters to my ex
I guess,
Maybe, I don't know,
I'm still holding onto hope
That goodbye wasn't for forever
And that we'll be together
At some point in the future from today

Or maybe it's just a way
To cope.
With the lingering love
that longs for a recipient.
Because in some ways I'm just writing to a
ghost
Penning my reflections to a figment of my
imagination,
Watering soil that once was home to a living
organism

At least I leave fertile ground for resurrection.

# bittersweet

8

Had I never had a taste
Of a sweet sample of love
Its full flavours and rich undertones

I'm sure I'd be better off

Because
Now I'm left with the bitter aftertaste.
Clinging to my tongue
Tainting my tastebuds
No matter how hard I try to wash it down

# Stolen water

I store these stolen moments in a piggy bank
One day I'll break it open and spend the years of
waiting.

I wonder if it will be worth it.

On second, sober thought.
Something tells me my stolen stores won't
amount to much at all
That they'll be eclipsed by the fullness of all this
love was meant to amount to.

I know it will be worth it.

# To those who wait

I'm learning a lesson in letting go
In the maybe but
Not now.
I'm finding out how virtuous patience can really
be.
Wait and see
Says the One who is the giver of gifts

Good things surely come

# Love actually

I pray our love lasts longer than the pages of a
notebook
Strong enough to stand when summer lovin'
faces winter's wind.
I pray that dancing in the dark translates to
walking in the light
When the music fades and the night draws to a
close.

We'll never be eighteen again.
And that's okay,
May what we have be beautified by time.

In between the flames of first love and the fine
wine of years together,
I pray we learn the steadfast sound of a repeated
refrain.
A song of sacrifice sung again and again
Because deep in the mundane
Remaining faithful day to day
Is where love actually is made.

# Still

Clear streams of air become a gentle wheeze
Silent streams of saline from squinted eyes glide
down chiselled cheeks
Tracing their way across a face whose owner is
Faced with the realities of their own feelings

A mind full of questions
A heart of flesh full of stones
A stomach starved and groaning
Not knowing with what it should be filled

Still

Peace is found in the stillness
In the willingness to wait
For the tide to subside
Because it does.

It always does.

# A True Story

I'm going back over my story
Revisiting the moments that I missed
The chapters that I skipped as I skimmed across
the surface of my own storyline.
At last the pages passed are being analysed
The pain pricks sharp as the the point of a pen
piercing paper
Each word a scar, yes faded, but still present
A part of my organic matter, meshed into my
skin

Maybe I was ignoring them, simply because I
could no longer feel the sensations of my
suffering
But here they were
Clear as day
Loud as pain
Endured without emotion

Now, I don't know
if these scars will ever go.
But now I find purpose interspersed between the
perforations
And beauty in what I once deemed disfiguration
A new interpretation of a well told tale

I understand now.
That even those moments that weren't planned
but were permitted
Fit perfectly into a greater narrative.
One I had to change my perspective to see,
Move my mind to perceive
And allow my heart to believe.

Truth that set my heart free.

# Under construction

I have a scar on my right shin.
Running my finger down my leg, I think about how
My skin still sinks in
Six years later,
The concave shape reminding me of a silly mistake
Made aged thirteen.

It's funny.
Each day I slip and I trip anew
As I feel my way through
The twisting paths of life.
But rarely do my mistakes make marks that last
So when they do
The moment is made that little bit more
Memorable

But.
Big or small.
I'm learning that slips are inevitable,
Perfection never reached this side of eternity

And yet, with all my faults and flaws,
My Maker calls me a masterpiece

Art still being painted
A sculpture still being formed.
A work in progress,
In the hands of One who won't stop
Until the work is done.

# New

There are times when I can't run to a friend
Moments when my might won't suffice in
carrying the weight
Rage that makes me shake, heartbreak or
heartache
So deep that it feels as though I'm drowning.

So I choose to project my pain to a Person who
gives infinite love yet knows infinite suffering
A Friend who takes my burden in exchange for a
change of mind
I find that that is all I really need

A mind renewed
A mind made
New

# Leaky vessels

We often give based on what we have received.
I hope we are leaky enough vessels to not
perpetuate the lacks we lived with
And instead have strength to become who we
needed.

Broken vessels that let the light shine through.

# on the train to grimsby

always on the move
but somehow stuck in the shackles of the same
situations
I know cycles can be stopped
and chains can be broken
but the process of disruption
can cause dysfunction for a season

ah well

a muscle torn is restored
even stronger than before.

and the heart's the strongest muscle of them all

# Elastic love

I want a heart that's big and stretchy
That moulds into the shape required to
accommodate
The souls of orphans

I want a heart that's healed, even if it still feels
the scars that pass on lessons

I want a heart that's thankful
Always ready to count the blessings despite the
stresses

I want a heart that holds a fire that heats a home
for hope

One that houses love that suffers long and bears
without complaint and never paints another in
the light of pain

I want a heart that's always ready to give and
overflows with more to spare
Full of tender mercies and joy and genuine care

Above all, let my heart be soft, soil for seeds of
truth and grace

Lord, hear my prayer because I know soft hearts
don't break.

# Cloud watching

I used to try to live in the clouds
But I found that their
Fluffy form can't perform the role of the ground
So now I simply gaze at what I used to find my
place in
Admiring the beauty,
But knowing deep down that to live in insecurity
Is equivalent to falling from the sky

# The surgeon's pen

My heart feels lighter after writing this
I'm certain that I'll once again play this role of a
surgeon

With my scalpel a pen
That cuts away the cancerous thoughts
Now displayed powerless on a page

See they're only malignant when trapped inside
the mind,
So I've learnt not to internalise,
Not allowing them to grow

My hope is that perhaps some of these words
can be
A remedy to the ailment of another.
That in some way by baring our burdens
We bear each others
As if to say this is a space
Where ugly can be brought and beautified
Where mud is a place to play and not to drown
Where shame is the thing shunned not any
person

We cry for catharsis and yearn for release.

Lay aside every weight and pick up peace.

It's within reach.

# until I know.

25

Until I know the title
I keep writing

Until I know the end
I keep reading

Until I know the score
I keep fighting

Until I know the song
I keep singing

Until I know the steps
I keep dancing

Until I know the fruit
I keep planting

Until I know the how
I keep trusting

Until I know the when
I keep hoping

Until I know the race is won

I must keep on running

Then I will know
That all I have done
Had its time and its place and its purpose

And all will be worth it.